broken fragments of my heart
or
mental illness killed me

by noori caiya

AF190146

noori caiya

For everyone who feels alone
with their problems.

For the teenagers with unsupportive parents.

For you.

Bibliografische Information der Deutschen Nationalbibliothek: Die Deutsche Nationalbibliothek verzeichnet diese Publikation in der Deutschen Nationalbibliografie; detaillierte bibliografische Daten sind im Internet über dnb.dnb.de abrufbar.

Herstellung und Verlag:
BoD – Books on Demand, Norderstedt

ISBN: 9783746078120

Hey you,

Before you start reading:
I know that this life is hard and sometimes
You wish you weren't here.
But the universe needs you.
I need you.
Even though you may not see your own future
I do.
And it is great.
It's a bright future that is ahead of you.
I hope you're not going to miss out on it.
Your pets would not understand were you left to.
Your mom would probably lay down on your bed at night
And wish she could say "good night" one more time.
Your siblings would miss you, annoying them.
Your best friend would have to sit through
School with your chair being empty.
I know it is tough but you can do it.
Just one more day:
We are doing baby steps okay?!
Just remember,
Baby steps until we are okay.
You are loved <3

He loved you more than anything in this world
He was consumed by your whole being
He got lost in your eyes
And stopped breathing when you laughed
He wanted you to be his forever
But you
You didn't care
You left him like it was the
Easiest thing in the world
But you didn't just leave him
You broke him
You broke him into
A million little pieces
That could not be fixed
He wanted to live
But you left nothing to live for
His love had nowhere to go
So, he wrote love on his arms
He drew butterflies
A million little butterflies
That show his love for you

Feeling is too much
I try to avoid feeling anything, which is depressing
How sad it is to live and not feel
But feeling hurts
It's uncomfortable
Every emotion is a color
They all mix together to a rainbow
And that rainbow is pressing against my skin
From the inside
I think I might explode
If I feel too much
And feeling little is not possible for me
So, I try to feel nothing

It's hard talking about your feelings when you
Don't know what you're feeling
It's a complete disaster in my head
As if a hurricane went through it

I wish you could look into my head to see
For I don't have the words
It's chaos
Painful chaos
I wish somebody would understand

I shed so many tears
I'd drown if the door was closed
But here she is
Opening the door
Every single time
Giving me love
Showing me I'm worthy

-thank you <3

You're still here, you know?
After everything you've been through
You're still standing
You're still out there doing your best
And if your best is just staying alive
That's enough
I'm proud of you
For fighting
For staying
For being

-I love you, beautiful human being <3

Books were a greater home to me than any
Place on earth could ever be
The magic, the love, the life
You can be whoever you want to
Someone you can't be in real life
It's nice sometimes
Being someone else
Seeing something else
Without actually having to leave

I fall in love with fictional characters
The traumatized and broken ones
The ones seen as a villain
Maybe because I know they'd understand me
They would hug me if I was sad and
They would always be there because
They know what it feels like
Yeah, they did bad things but they would
Burn down the world so I could be happy

I want somebody to love me like that
To be someone's world

Mental illnesses are real
Yeah, it's in the head
But the brain is still an organ
The brain is ill
Mental illnesses are serious
For they end in death sometimes

I love getting tattoos
The pain
It's soothing
My mind is quiet then
And the pain...
Oh, how I love the pain

I say I'm clean
But if I'm being honest with myself
I'm not
I don't drag a blade across my skin
But I'm not clean either
Self-harm is more than cutting

I like to pretend
I'm dying
Not really, but in my mind
Just for a minute
So, I get to pause
Only for a moment
From a life that takes too much

The mirror betrays me
It shows me something that isn't true
I avoid looking at it
Looking at me through it
For it whispers in my ear
I'm not beautiful

Mental illness killed me
And I don't mean the body I live in
It killed everything that made me who I am
I don't laugh like I used to
I don't see the world as colorful as I used to
And I don't like being around people anymore
Mental illness took a part of me and
I don't think I'll ever get it back

My parents took a lot of time making my heart
And gosh it's beautiful
Not for a lot of people
But for some
And for me
They took the time to make it out of glass so
The sun could shine into it and
Reflect in a colorful rainbow over the world

Glass breaks quite easily
And it did
It absolutely shattered into pieces
My heart cuts me from the inside
Sometimes it feels like dying

But you know what?
The pieces make an even more beautiful rainbow
Than they did when they were a whole

I want you
I want "us"
I want to try "us"
But I don't want you to leave
Over and over again
I don't want to miss you and
I don't want you to take my heart with you
I want to be present in my world here
Don't want to think about you being away
In your own world

I often think about "us"
And what we could've been
If life didn't get in the way
If life didn't decide it would be best
To live apart
If life chose us to be an "us"
I'm sure we would've been great together
But here we are
Me being me and you being you
With no "us" even close
We're both living in our world
Apart from the "us"

-long distance love

It's so exhausting making plans for your future
When you don't want to be alive
When you have to decide what job you want to do
For the rest of your life
For a life you don't even want to have
It's so overwhelming and I'm tired
I don't want to make these decisions
I'm already out of energy and I don't know
How even to manage working 8 hours a day
I'm mentally drained to the point
Where I can't work without having mental breakdowns
I need more time
But there isn't more time

You still wander in my brain sometimes
It's like you come by for a visit
To check if I'm still out there doing okay
And that hurts
Because I want you
I want you so bad
But I know it'll only hurt more if I allow myself
To love you

You told me I'm not an unlovable person
Nobody ever told me that before and now
I can't stop thinking about it
How dare you tell me that and then leave

You were born on a cliff
To fall
You were born with wings
To fly
You were born with the ability
To choose

I go blind to the outside sometimes
Because my brain is playing a movie of its own
A movie of the horrible things you did
The way you touched me and I let you
Because I was afraid
The way I kept my mouth shut
Because I was afraid
The way you permanently burned this in my brain
Because I was afraid
The way I was afraid
Afraid of you
Afraid to speak
My silence was a "no"
But you read it as "yes"
And I blamed myself for it
Because I was too afraid

Words drip
From the tip of my pen
Onto the sheet
Words
My mouth didn't dare
To speak

Fear is a poison
It settles in your veins and
Slowly bleeds through your skin
Until it reaches your vital organs
When those are infected
There is no turning back
Fear is a part of you now
And you have to find a way
To control it
So, it doesn't control you

"You have to find a way
To shut down the voices in your head"
The voices are me and I am the voices
I'd have to kill me to kill the voices

I scraped my knees and burned my skin
Crawling through hell
So, you better believe I'm not giving up
I AM hell
I'm your worst nightmare
Burn me down as much as you like
But fire is what I am made out of now

Yeah, struggling with mental illness is tough
And I wish I wasn't
But seeing people you love battle those demons
Fucks you up on another level
To know they're holding on for dear life
But still walk around laughing, seemingly happy
Like damn, I just wish I could take away your pain
I don't care about my pain
But you...
I don't want to see you hurt like this

Red was my favorite color as a kid
Now I despise the look of red
As its painting my eyes
Through the tears
Now I despise the look of red
As its dripping down my sleeves
Through the pain

Swimming is an escape
I don't feel the weight of the world
And when I'm underwater it's so unbelievably calm
It fascinates me how close to death I am
If I just stopped coming up for air
I like how it feels when I'm short of air
And should come up, but don't
The fuzziness in my brain
And the thoughts slowing down
It's relaxing

I don't like to tell people I write
I rather keep it a secret
It's the pressure that comes within
That keeps me from speaking about it
The pressure of being good
That I can articulate in a remarkable way
And am well-spoken because
"Writers need a good vocabulary"
I don't have that
Sometimes I can't even communicate
My own needs and feel like all the letters
Are being mixed up or don't come out at all
I'm not good with words
And people don't seem to understand
How those things go together
To be honest I don't either
The pressure keeps me from talking
About what I really like

-the pressure of being an artist

I feel like I haven't quite been
A good person in a while and
Maybe that's why I don't deserve to be loved
I'm fine with that
But the happy, little child inside of me
Deserves to be loved
For she did nothing wrong
She always was a good person

The artist inside me always existed
The way I let the pen glide over the paper
When I was feeling too much
It was a freeing feeling
Depression took over the artist in me
For the pen is a blade now
And the paper is my skin

I wish people on this earth wouldn't be so cruel
I wish people wouldn't comment on my body
I wish people wouldn't stare at my scars
I wish people wouldn't talk about me for looking "weird"
I wish people wouldn't call me stupid things
I wish people wouldn't look at me disgusted
I wish people wouldn't change seats when they see my
rainbow flag
I wish people would just mind their own business

-being a mentally ill queer

I want to go to sleep
Because it's like dying
Without actually dying
It makes life bearable
I just don't want to be awake
When my own thoughts are attacking me

I don't want to go to sleep
Because then my thoughts are hunting me
As nightmares without the barrier of reality
So, it's even worse

I can't stand being awake
I can't stand being asleep
There is no escape from my mind anymore

I said its okay that you're gone
And it is... but I'm not
I'm absolutely not okay
I avoid looking at old pictures and videos
I try to distract myself
So, my mind doesn't have a chance
To think about you
But sometimes a memory
Slips into my consciousness and it hits me
Like a brick
The pain
The emptiness
Its unbearable
It feels like my lungs cave in and
My head is spinning
But yes... it is okay that you're gone
I just won't be okay for some time
I guess even that is okay

Things you maybe need to hear:

It's normal to be exhausted after a panic attack
Your body went through a tremendous amount of stress
It's okay to rest afterwards

Its normal and okay to be tired after feeling a lot of
emotions
Even if you laid in bed all day, emotions are tiring too

Healing isn't a linear process; Steps back are normal

You're not lazy for staying in bed all day
Your body and brain need to rest

You're doing a great job
I'm proud of you for waking up today
I'm proud of you for sticking around
You are loved <3

Stay alive
Eat something, you deserve it
Stay hydrated
Rest well
Don't stress yourself

Why is nobody talking about how
Mentally exhausting transitioning is?
You don't know your own body anymore
Everything is changing
People act different
The constant fear of being outed
And assaulted
The fear of bullying
And abandonment
People finding out your deadname
Surgery
Relationships are changing because so are you
Having to explain everything to everyone
Questions about what's in your pants

-being trans

I kind of like the way self-harm effects my body
The way this perfect, clean spot of skin gets ruined
Of its perfection
The way it makes my body less perfect
Uglier I assume
More like the way I feel inside
Ugly
Absolutely not perfect
And damaged
I like my imperfect, self-made tattoos
For the same reason
People think they're ugly and make me ugly
But why would I want people to only love me
If I have a perfect body when my soul is not
And it's about personality anyway?

"I'm sorry for your loss"
Heard that a few times by now
I don't know what to answer
"I'm doing okay" or
"I'm doing terrible"
Because I am doing both at the same time
I mean I am okay I guess
I'm slowly getting better and
My happiness is coming back
But on the other hand, I'm doing so terrible
I don't even know the words to my feelings

Suddenly the world got so quiet
Like it's missing your voice
The same moment it got so loud
And overwhelming
The hole where your voice was
Left an echo storming through my mind
Only getting louder

I want to lay in your lap
And cry like a child that
Scraped its knee
I want you to hold me and tell me
Everything will be alright
That the sun will shine again
And life will be good
That the pain will end
And I will find my smile again

I want the world to notice my pain
When nobody does and the pain is
Unbearable to handle alone
My brain tells me to hurt myself
Not to speak but
To hurt myself
So, when you see me covered in wounds
Just know that the pain is
Too much to handle

It's like a craving for ice cream
You know it'll make you feel good
And oh, how bad it is staring at you from the fridge
At first you simply can say no and move on
But with every minute it's getting harder to resist
Until its almost physically impossible
You start to feel the pain in your body
And it's the only thing you can think about
No matter what you do
It's always the next thought
And as soon as you say
"Just one more time"
You lost

Every time I hit a rock bottom
I crave to feel the numbness
I know how to achieve it
And it feels so damn good
It's just clouds in my head
And no more demons
I want to feel like that
My soul is craving it
And it's painful
The weight on my soul
I could erase
With one single move
But I can't
Because it's wrong

The worst part
About waking up the next morning
Is not what you feel
On the inside
It's the part
Where you have to look into the mirror
Into your own eyes and realize
Nothing's changed
You are in the same position
You were in 24 hours ago
Everything is the same
Life goes on
After your attempt

I don't want to die
I just want the pain to stop
I can't live with this pain anymore
And the knowledge it won't get better
Cause it's a lifelong thing

-borderline bipolar

It burns to shower
You may not know what I mean
And that's fine
I wish for you to not understand
When the darkness hits and
I am suffocating in my own thoughts
The only-thing that helps
Is the silver across my skin
The relief afterwards as if
The darkness leaves me
Through the cuts I made
Like I bleed it out
The stinging pain scares the clouds away
And I can finally think clear again
And then the regret hits you
Because it is wrong
To do things that hurt you
Things that only make it worse
Over time

A stranger
Leaning against the wall
In front of me
Someone with their own life
And their own thoughts
And I wonder
What touches this person's heart?
Or more specific what
Broke their heart?
What made them this person?
This person that goes to a park
Alone in the middle of the night
Listening to music on full blast
Pain written all over their face
Hands trembling
Memories flashing through their head

Maybe it was a mirror
I was looking into
But regardless
All I see is a stranger
Pain written all over their face

Sleepy eyes
Are staring back at me
When I look into the mirror
Exhausted eyes
Tired of fighting
Sad eyes
Tired of crying
Eyes with no life
Are what I see

I remember the time
You told me you wished
You were dead
My happy little heart shattered
Right there on the stairs
I couldn't grasp it

And now
Now I can't let it go
The wish to be dead
Myself

A soft crunch under my feet
With every step the snow gets deeper
And I have to fight harder to keep going
I can't stop or else my time is up
I don't want to give up
I want to get out of this snowstorm
Into the sun
I want to feel the warmth on my skin
I want the summer back
But I'm stuck in this mess
And it's getting harder to breath
There is a lot of pain
I'm also numb at the same time
My feet stop and
I sink backwards into the snow
Heavy breaths leave my lungs
As I stare at the grey clouds above me
No more fight is left in me
My eyes close slowly and
I can feel a sunray tickle my face
With its warmth
Is the summer coming to save me?

Its 3am
My bed feels like a soft cloud
Embracing me in itself
And I begin to think of you
Every laughter we shared
And all the fights we had
I saw us grow old together
But I guess it wasn't meant to be
I wonder if you lay awake
Like I do
Or if you are sound asleep
I once read that
If you are awake at 3am
You are either lonely or in love
And now I'm questioning
Myself which one it is today

It hurts me to see how well you are doing
Now that I'm gone
You are thriving and living your best life
You are kind to the people around you
And you seem really happy
And yes of course
I want all that for you
I only want the best for you
Because I still love you
That doesn't change the fact that it hurts
It really hurts
Because it makes me feel
As if I was the problem all along
Was I the problem all along?

I could try and explain to you
How you broke me and
What pain you brought me
But I know how it would end
So, I'm being the reasonable one
And am leaving

When you're in a room
And suddenly the light turns off
You start looking for the light switch,
A flashlight or the door
You start moving through the darkness
Slowly but steady
And you will find something
You just have to start searching
The light is always near

Nothing is ever enough
So, if you've given your all
And they still chose someone else
Set them free
Some people are meant to be a page
Or a chapter but not the whole book
It's time to continue reading
Your story isn't over

Healing is hard
It seems like a huge mountain
You know the view will be amazing
Once you reached to top
But from the ground
You only see the hard path
In front of you

The worst part about being loved
Is realizing it's not going to heal you
All the wounds are still hurting
And the sadness doesn't leave

You have to find your own happiness
And heal your own wounds
Because no one ever will be able
To do that for you
Love just gives you someone
That holds your hand
Whilst you are healing

You were always by my side
When I was losing myself

But now I lost you
And found myself

If I could choose a superpower
I'd always choose being invisible
But nobody understands why
Just like nobody gets why women
Are terrified to go out alone or in the dark
You only get it if you know how it feels
And I do
I know how it feels
To walk down a street and
Getting stared at like a creep
I know how it feels
To be helpless and being terrified
You're not going to come home tonight
I know how it feels
To say, „NO" but they don't listen
I know how it feels
When this happens at a young age
I know how it feels
When you can't forget about it
I know how it feels
To be a woman

Sadness feels like drowning
Happiness feels like exploding
Anxiety feels like dying
And anger feels like murder

There is no normal state of emotion
It's either feeling this
Or nothing

You told me you love me forever
And I did too
The difference is that your forever ended
And mine didn't
Now my love is lost on the moon
It couldn't come back
Because you're not here anymore
It searches for you again and again
But you're on airplane mode
Not available

When I was 13 years old
My biology teacher taught me
That some flowers change their color to red
After they have been pollinated
After they have been used
To show that nothing was left

And now I realize
That's the same with humans
After they have been used
Their eyes turn red from crying
And you know nothing is left

Sometimes gravity is my enemy
It keeps me in a place
I don't belong
A place I don't want to be in
But I am not able to fly to the moon
Without a rocket

„Why are you doing it?"
I don't know, I replied
I knew
I knew exactly why I did it
To feel something for once
To feel that I am still alive
And that the pain in my heart
Is not that bad
That it can heal
Like my body can
To treat the physical pain
Because I can't do it
With the pain in my heart
To get help
To get noticed
I wanted somebody to notice
That I didn't know what to do anymore
That I was lost and broken
That I couldn't handle this life anymore
But how do you tell someone
Who thinks you are doing okay
That you aren't fine on your own

You know that
If I should not wake up tomorrow
The sun still shines
The earth still turns and
The moon still watches out for you
The universe may have lost a star
But it's still the universe in its whole
I am just a star
One from billions
It may seem a little darker
But there is plenty light out there
So go find it
Your new light
Promise me you will

It's like being underwater
Everything is quiet and blurry
You don't really seem to be a part
Of the world anymore
Like you're floating in your own bubble
But it feels safe
Warm
Comfortable
It's an escape
Your own little planet
Away from the darkness
And the pain

-dissociation

A puddle on the ground
I see my reflection in it
A complete mess
I don't even recognize myself anymore
Dark circles under my eyes
Dried tears on my cheeks
And no emotions left
The moonlight is shining down on me
And I am lost
There's a fire in my soul
And it is burning
It is burning everything to the ground
It is getting out of control
Everything I built for myself
Everything I accomplished
Is breaking down
Every wound that healed
Is opening again
My thoughts got blown by the wind
And my emotions are scrambled
All over the concrete

Dear Mama,
I know life is hard and I wish
I never found out the way I did
But I just want to say sorry
I'm sorry
For the sleepless nights you had
While I couldn't sleep
I'm sorry
For all the tears I brought you
Because I said something bad again
I'm sorry
For every fight we had
Because I know I hurt you
I'm sorry
For all the fear you had
While watching me fight depression
I'm sorry
For all the pain you went through
When I cried and didn't want you near me
But I am thankful
For all the things you went through
Because they kept me going

I'm destroying myself
That's what they all tell me
All day long
When I can't get out of bed
Or do my chores
When I don't feel like going to school
Or doing my homework
When I just want to be on my phone
To escape reality for a while
To make it all stop for a while
I'm destroying myself
Yeah, maybe I am
But isn't it better to damage myself a bit
now than to end it all and
Never get the chance to live my life?!
Because I want to live my life
But right now, I need to "destroy" myself
To be able to survive

I am tired of explaining my problems
Or why I am the way I am
I am tired of telling strangers
Who get paid to listen to me
Why I feel sad
What quirks I have
I am tired of talking
Please let me sit in silence
And understand me just the same

I'm okay with the scars
That cover my body
But sometimes I forget
They will stay forever
They will always tell their story

I never thought I would reach
This point in my life
I really thought I could handle it
All the shit that happened and still does
I always told myself that I need no distraction
and I can live with the pain
But now
Now I'm nearly at my breaking point
I just want to feel nothing for a while
Don't exist and don't feel the pain
The suffering
The suffocating thoughts
And the voices in my head
I want to feel it burning down my throat
And making a warm, fuzzy feeling in
My stomach
The liquor I always highly respected
It has a power I was afraid of
But now I want to abuse this power
And make it all okay for a while

My heart isn't broken
It is shattered into a million pieces
And these pieces turned into dust
And the dust got blown away
And I just don't know anymore

I have a blue friend
He is always by my side when I feel lonely
He visits at my darkest times
He talks to me and tries to help me
We grow more and more together

My dear blue friend
I always thought
You were the best for me
You made it seem
But now that the light is back in my life
I realize
You never were my friend

So, my dear blue
Please stay away from me
You tried to take my life

My dear blue
You are my suicide

The system fails a lot of teenagers
The ones who need help
Who struggle with mental illness
Who are lost and broken

Because social workers or
So called professionals
Always chose their own comfort
Over their clients well being

I'm not just a case
I am a human being
With feelings and rights

If you can't even treat me
like a decent human being
You're failing at you job
Miserably

Social work
You study for years
Work for years
And yet
You manage to lose
Your human instincts
Your common sense
Your heart
And fail miserably in your job

-so called professionals

I clench my jaw and hold my breath
I don't want to let go
Don't want to lose control
Cause if I did
I would ruin the world I built
My anger spreads
Through my veins and
Reaches every part of my body
I am mad and hurt
I am mad because I am hurt
Because you hurt me
And I thought you never would
I trusted you with my life and
You let me down
You have proven your point
You made it clear
The hate you have for me
The pain I brought you
And my pain turned into anger
Anger that makes it hard to forgive you
Anger that hurts people around me
Anger that hurts me

I wanted to talk
I still do
But I knew you wouldn't understand
So, I kept quiet and let you talk
In hope
You would maybe understand
My silence
...
You never did

I can picture your lifeless body
Thin, broken
I could see every bone and
the dark circles under your eyes
I saw how your smile faded away
Day after day
I saw you stepping
Closer to the edge
But couldn't do anything
Death was grabbing after you
And I felt it
I felt it every second
And I was afraid
Because I couldn't change it
I could just watch, wait and hope
And now I see it again
The monster
I can see it, even though this time
I know it is not there
But in my head, it is
I can't tell the difference

Your touch
I still feel your fingertips
On my skin
I still feel like I'm trapped
Under your bodyweight
I still hear your laugh
Echoing through the room
I still feel you
You
How thought you did nothing wrong
You
How you just wanted to make a joke
You
How you never wanted to hurt me
You
How you still did

-triggering a trauma

I am a tree
You can hurt me and rip my branches of
You can rip out my roots
You can pick my flowers
And give them away
You can carve your
Mistaken love into me
You can make me bleed
You can burn me to the ground
You can force me to be furniture
I will get all wrinkly
And one day I will die

No matter how much you hurt or shape me
I will always be a tree

I am the unwanted extra
The bit that nobody wanted
I made your life so much harder
And you only punished me for it
For not being perfect
For needing help
He got your help but
You didn't see I needed it too
I needed you to help me
To love me
To accept me
I just needed you

Art has always been a part of me
And shall I die, my darling
I'd paint the sky
In the most ravishing colors

I am dying
For life isn't one for me
At times it is hard
To find something
So bright and worthy
It makes you want to live

Pain is easy
To see through the pain
When that's all you see
Is the real art
Of life

I don't know about in 10 years
In 5 years
In a year
A month
Or a week
I don't even know about tomorrow
So tell me
How am I supposed to know
My whole future
What job I want
If I want kids
Or even who I am
...
I don't
So let me figure it out
On my own

I want to live
But I also want to die
I mean I have a lot to live for
So many things I want to experience
But on the other hand
There's this pain
And I just want it to stop
I know it won't
So I sit and wish
For my last breath to come

That's probably selfish
Because many people have it worse
But I can't keep telling myself that

I won't end my life
But if it were to end now
I wouldn't be mad

What if
I am not strong enough
To win
Against my own thoughts?
What if
I lose this fight?

The issue isn't the darkness itself
It's what lives within
That terrifies me
When I'm most vulnerable

I crave intimacy
Simple acts of love and kindness
But I avoid it
Since it has been to long
And I am afraid I might break
Once someone touches
My skin made of porcelain

The cup of poison
We are drinking from
Is the one
We poisoned ourselves

When you're in a storm
You seemingly can't escape
A storm that's tearing you apart
Find it's center
For it is quiet in the
Eye of the hurricane

Some people
Pour their entire hearts
Standing in a puddle
Of their own blood
Simply to be understood

The dust is my friend
He is my companion
In the loneliness
He dances in the wind
Also sparkles in the sun
He never leaves my side
And if I were to never move again
He'd hug me
Until I've decomposed
To dust
For we can dance together
From now on

I never learned how to speak
So I taught myself
Silence
The language of the unspoken mind
A language nobody seems to speak
But me

Pain is a beautiful source of art
You want art
Search for pain
Every artist carries pain within

I read in order to survive
Because someone else's pain
Is lighter than my own
Someone else's mind
Is a better place to be

Pins and needles
Fill my limbs
Crawling through my skin
Once my body disconnects
With my mind
And I am not me anymore
The body is left
But I am gone

-depersonalization

I write and write and write
In order to forget you
To get you out of my system
Your infectious self
But when my eyes scan
The words I've written
All I see is your name

I would slit all my veins open
And bleed out every ounce of blood
That is contained in my body
If it meant for you to be truly happy
I would take all the pain in the world
For you to never feel pain again

We are growing up
And that means we're changing
For the better and worse
But for some reason
I never thought
We are going to change
In different directions

I told my mom about you
I told her I really liked you
And she was happy
She was happy I found someone

I don't know how to tell her
We don't exist anymore
That we don't like each other anymore
That I'm alone again

You changed me you know?!
Not my personality or the way I look
But you gave me memories
Memories I will always remember
Stuff that's stuck with me
I will think of you
When I watch a Marvel movie
Because you loved Bucky so much
I will think of you
When I see people smoke
Because you always did
I will think of you
Throughout my life
Because a part of you stays after all

I dance on rooftops
to the music that screams in my head
I climb on the highest trees
With no way back
I drink the strongest liquor
With no friend around
I lose myself in this heavy world
No matter how far I go
No matter how close I come
I still can't find a way to live
With all this pain

If your heart is still bleeding
Like mine
Come sit with me
In silence we can bleed
Together
My brother in pain

Mama
I know you said to write
When it pains
And I assure you I do
I write so hard my fingers break
And my skin cracks open
I write with the blood you gave me
I fear I might bleed myself dry
With all the pain I carry inside

It's killing me
This whole life thing
It's killing me
Slowly
Steadily
And painful
But it's killing me
And I don't mean in the
"You're born and will die someday" way
But more in the
"I'm in so much pain and
Life just seems like a huge burden
I can't deal with for much longer" way

I have all these voices inside me
Screaming
Loud and scary
...
Yes, I am scared
Terrified even
Of my own mind
A place I should feel safe in
A place that should be my home
But it isn't
It never actually was
And I want to leave
But I don't have elsewhere to go
I am scared
I want them to stop
Please make them stop

When I learned one thing in life it's:
Never to give up on yourself
You can and will lose
Everybody in your life eventually
Might it be through a break-up
Or later death
Everyone will leave at some point
Except for you
You have yourself until
The very last second from
The very first second
You have yourself
Through the hardest times
And the most joyful ones
Every single thing you will go through in life
Your body, your heart,
Your mind and your soul
Will always be there
They don't leave you
So never ever give up on yourself

Acknowledgments

Special thanks to my best friend who always supported me through all my highs and lows. Who never gave up on me even though I was not easy to be around sometimes. Thank you for not seeing me differently after coming out and thank you for being in my life <3

I am also grateful for my brother who let me be who I am and not once judged me for it. Who walked with me through the hardest paths of life. Who helped me see the light at the end of the tunnel. And whom I got writing from. As a child I was always fascinated and inspired from his writings. So, thank you for showing me this whole new world.

Also lets not forget my parents who made it possible for me to be here by giving birth to me. Thank you for trying your hardest and not giving up on me.